Fruits

Contents

 Look and put the sticker.

strawberries

kiwis

peaches

bananas

 **Put sticker on the word.**

What fruit do you like?

I like bananas .

 Ask and say.

Color and say.

 strawberries

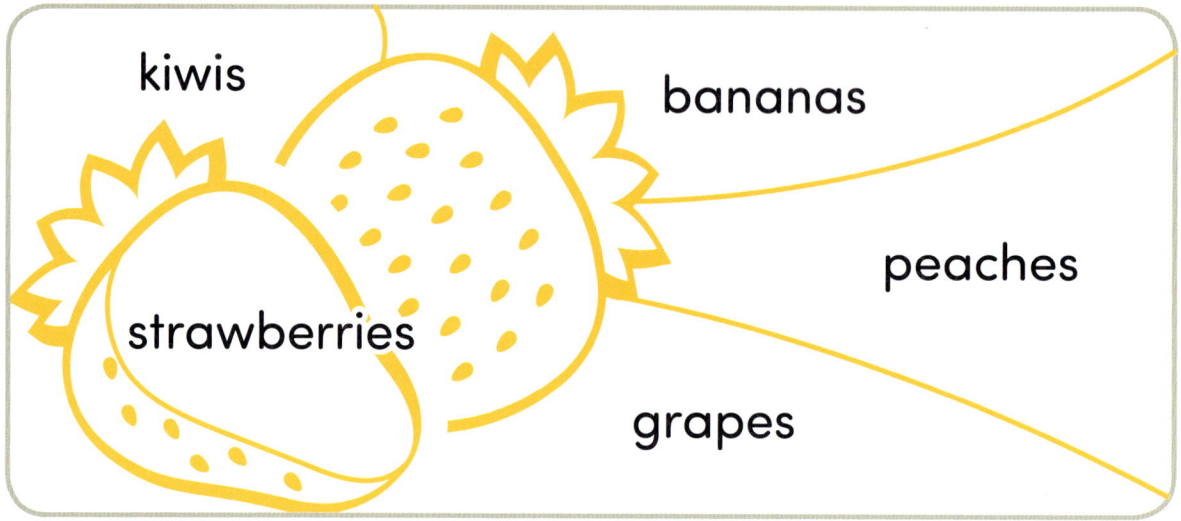

kiwis   bananas

peaches

strawberries

grapes

 peaches

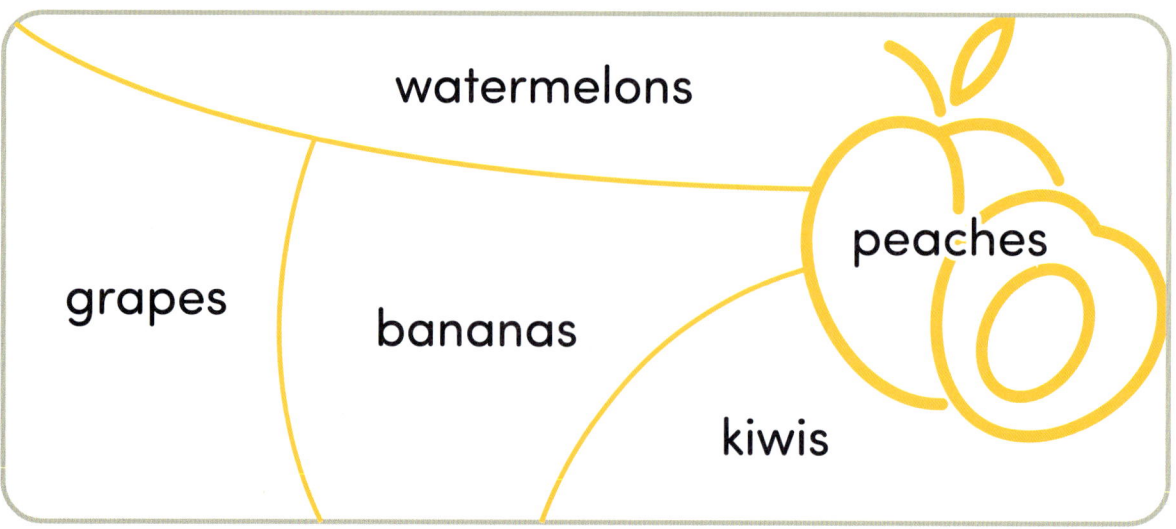

watermelons

peaches

grapes   bananas

kiwis

 Look and put the sticker.

watermelons

blueberries

grapes

oranges

 **Put sticker on the word.**

What fruit
do you like?

I like peaches .

 Ask and say.

Color.

watermelons

grapes

Let's Have Fun

Sticker

Put the fruits in his mouth.

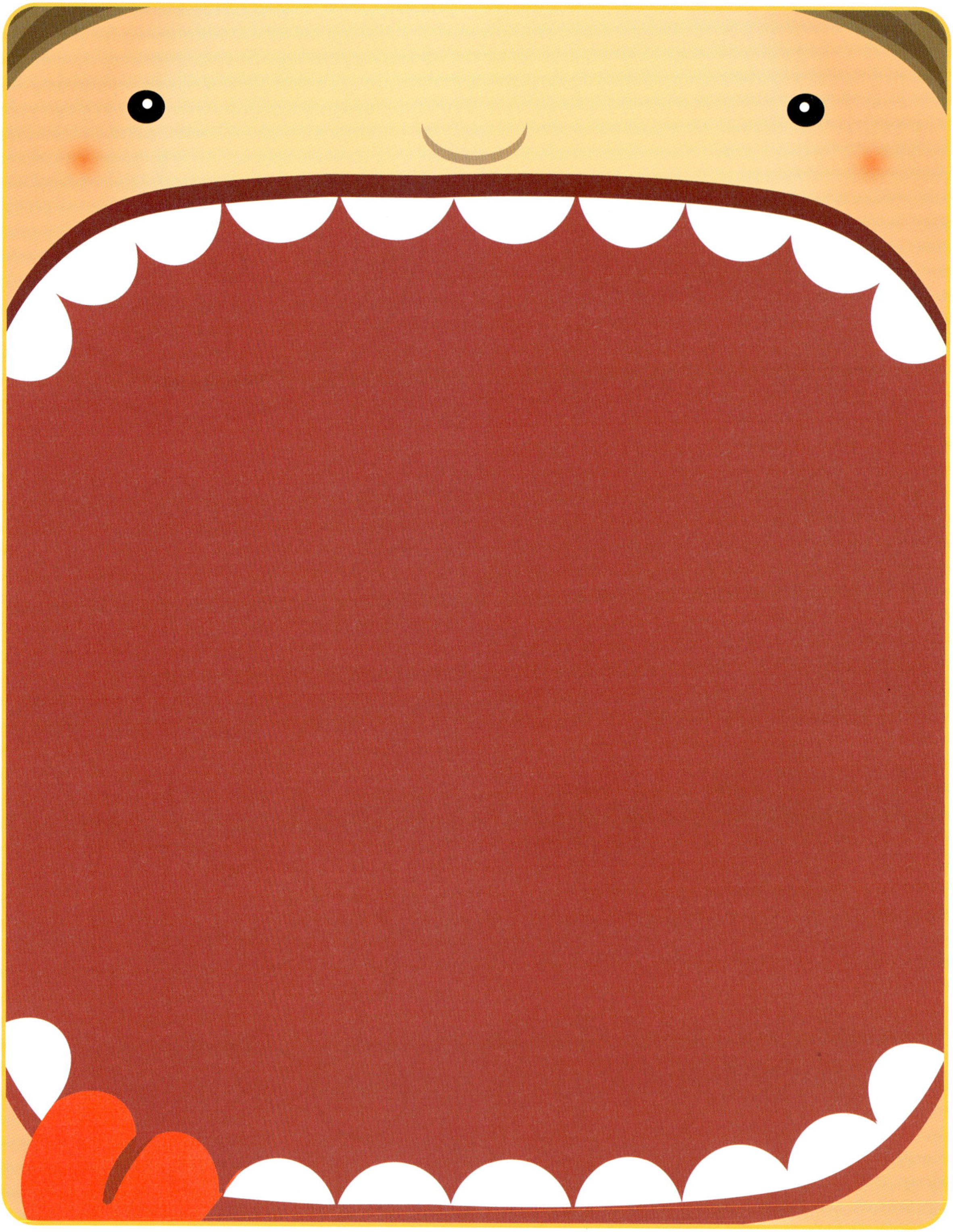

oranges peaches

grapes strawberries

| kiwis | blueberries |
| watermelons | bananas |